MW01118792

CATS

TABBY CATS

STUART A. KALLEN

ABDO & Daughters

Published by Abdo & Daughters, 4940 Viking Drive, Suite 622, Edina, Minnesota 55435.

Library bound edition distributed by Rockbottom Books, Pentagon Tower, P.O. Box 36036, Minneapolis, Minnesota 55435.

Copyright © 1996 by Abdo Consulting Group, Inc., Pentagon Tower, P.O. Box 36036, Minneapolis, Minnesota 55435 USA. International copyrights reserved in all countries. No part of this book may be reproduced in any form without written permission from the publisher.

Printed in the United States.

Cover Photo credit: Firth Photo Bank
Interior Photo credits: Peter Arnold, Inc. pages 5, 7, 9, 11, 15
Firth Photo Bank, pages 13, 17, 19, 21

Edited by Rosemary Wallner

Library of Congress Cataloging-in-Publication Data

Kallen, Stuart A., 1955
    Tabby cat / Stuart A. Kallen.
    p. cm. — (Cats)
Includes bibliographical references (p.24) and index.
    ISBN 1-56239-447-9
l. Tabby cats—Juvenile literature. [1. Tabby cats. 2. Cats.] I. Title. II. Series
Kallen, Stuart A., 1955- Cats.
SF449.T32K35   1995
636.8'2—dc20   95-10525
                                                      CIP
                                                      AC

ABOUT THE AUTHOR
Stuart Kallen has written over 80 children's books, including many environmental science books.

Contents

LIONS, TIGERS, AND CATS

THE MIDDLE EAST

Turkey

Lebanon

Israel

Syria

Iraq

Iran (Persia)

United Arab Emirates

Egypt

Jordan

Kuwait

Qatar

Saudi Arabia

Oman

Yemen

Few animals are as beautiful and graceful as cats. And all cats are related. From the wild lions of Africa to the common house cat, all belong to the family **Felidae**. Cats are found almost everywhere. They include cheetahs, jaguars, lynx, ocelots, and **domestic** cats.

People first **domesticated** cats about 5,000 years ago in the Middle East. Although humans have **tamed** them, house cats still think and act like their bigger cousins.

Cats are found almost everywhere. They include cheetahs, jaguars, lynx, ocelots, and domestic cats.

TABBY CATS

There are many different **breeds** of cat. But most cats are **non-pedigree**, sometimes called mutts, or "moggies." The most common type of non-pedigree cat has the markings of the tabby. Tabby markings are spots and stripes. This is the closest cats come to looking like leopards and tigers, their **ancient** relatives.

IRAQ

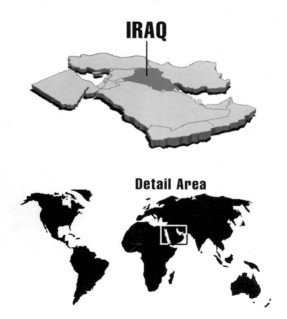

Detail Area

Tabby cats appear in **ancient** Egyptian artwork. The name "tabby" comes from Attabiya, a section of ancient Bagdad, a city in Iraq. In this part of the city, people made striped cloth. In Britain, people called this cloth "tabbi silk."

Tabby cats look like leopards and tigers, their ancient relatives.

WHAT THEY'RE LIKE

Today, many cats have at least some tabby-striped fur on them—no matter what their **breed**. Tabbies are basic, down-to-earth cats. They are smart, good-natured, and make the best sort of friend.

Tabby cats make great friends.

COAT AND COLOR

Tabbies come in many colors. They may be brown, silver, orange, or black. Their coat is short, dense, and crisp. Tabbies are well known for their stripes, rings, and necklace-like markings. The stripes on some tabbies are broken up into spots. Many tabbies have white paws or "boots."

These tabbies have silver coats.

SIZE

Tabbies are stocky, powerful cats. They have strong legs and a round head set on a muscular neck. Their large, round eyes may be copper, gold, hazel, or orange.

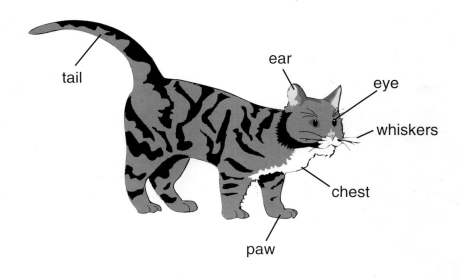

Most cats share the same features.

This tabby cat has large, round, gold eyes.

CARE

Common tabbies are used to taking care of themselves. But like all cats, tabbies love a good brushing. Besides making the cat purr, brushing a tabby will keep its loose hair off the furniture. **Grooming** a tabby will also keep **hair balls** from forming.

Like any pet, tabbies need love and attention. Cats make fine pets. But they still have some of their wild **instincts**.

Cats are natural hunters and do well exploring outdoors. A scratching post where the cat can sharpen its claws saves furniture from damage.

Cats bury their waste and should be trained to use a litter box. Clean the box every day. Cats love to play. A ball, **catnip**, or a loose string will keep a kitten busy for hours.

Tabbies need love and attention.

FEEDING

Cats eat meat and fish. Hard bones that do not splinter help keep the cat's teeth and mouth clean. Water should always be available. Most cats enjoy dried cat food. Kittens enjoy their mother's milk. However, milk can cause illness in full-grown cats.

Tabby cats eat fish and meat.

KITTENS

Female cats are **pregnant** for about 65 days. Litters range from two to eight kittens. The average cat has four kittens.

Kittens are blind and helpless for the first several weeks. After about three weeks, they will start crawling and playing. At this time they may be given cat food.

After about a month, kittens will run, wrestle, and play games. At 10 weeks, the kittens are old enough to be sold or given away.

Three weeks after being born, kittens start to crawl and play.

BUYING A KITTEN

You can buy tabbies at a pet store. People also sell cats in newspaper ads.

When buying a kitten, check it closely for signs of good health. The ears, nose, mouth, and fur should be clean. Eyes should be bright and clear. The cat should be alert and interested in its surroundings. A healthy kitten will move around with its head held high.

*A healthy tabby kitten will move
with its head held high.*

GLOSSARY

ANCIENT (AYN-chent) - Very old.

BREED - To raise or grow; also a group of animals that look alike and have the same type of ancestors.

CATNIP - A strong-smelling plant used as stuffing for cat toys.

DOMESTICATE (doe-MESS-tih-kate) - To tame or adapt to home life.

FELIDAE (FEE-lih-day) - The Latin name given to the cat family.

GROOMING - Cleaning and brushing.

HAIR BALLS - Balls of fur that gather in a cat's stomach after grooming itself by licking.

INSTINCT - A way of acting that is born in an animal, not learned.

NON-PEDIGREE - An animal without a record of its ancestors.

PREGNANT - With one or more babies growing inside the body.

TAME - To reduce from a wild to a domestic state.

Index

BIBLIOGRAPHY

Alderton, David. *Cats.* New York: Dorling Kindersley, 1992.

Clutton-Brock, Juliet. *Cat.* New York: Alfred A. Knopf, 1991.

DePrisco, Andrew. *The Mini-Atlas of Cats.* Neptune City, N.J.: T.F.H. Publications, 1991.

Taylor, David. *The Ultimate Cat Book.* New York: Simon & Schuster, 1989.